Verse from the Village

HYMN

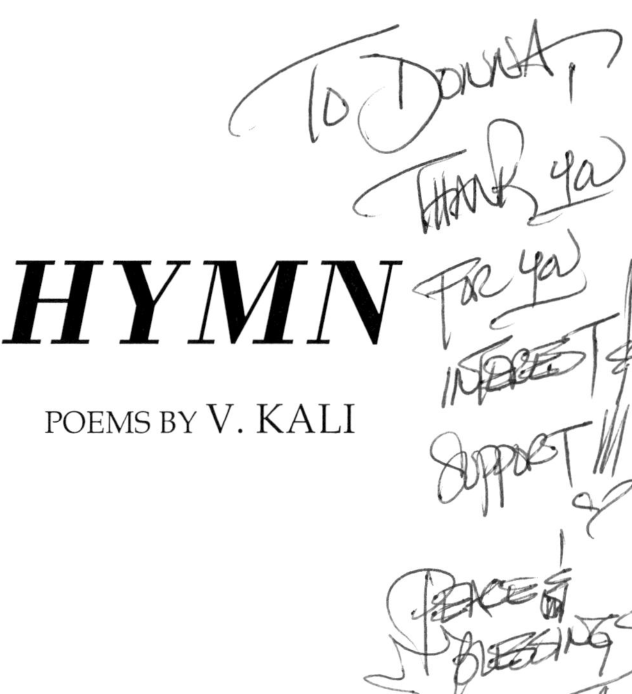

HYMN

POEMS BY V. KALI

World Stage Press
Verse from the Village

ISBN-13: 978-1540666796
ISBN-10: 1540666794

Printed in the United States of America

Layout Design: Nadia Hunter Bey
Cover Design: Undeniable Ink.
Cover Photo: John Byrd
Sketch: Billy Burgos
Last Page Photo: V. Kali

This is dedicated to Cedric James Hinson, and
lovers of HYMNS everywhere.

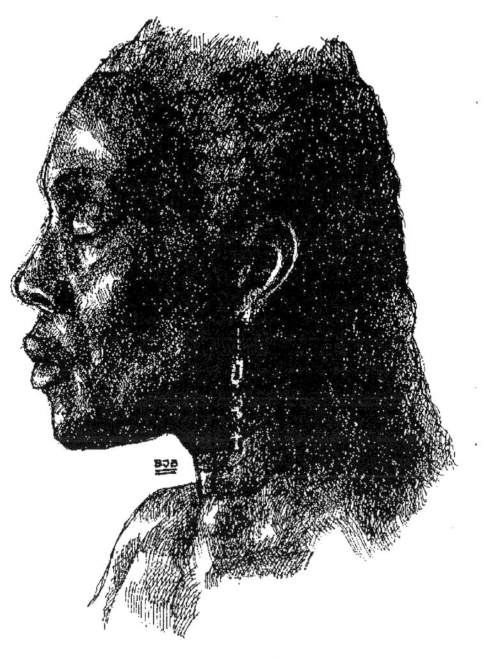

The Sacred, Brazen,
TABLE OF HYMNspiration

1ST TESTAMENT 16
WRITTEN ON THE NINE 17
HE SPEAKS 18
UNDER A JULY SKY 20
SPRINGTIME 21
RITUAL 22
COLLAGE A TROIS 23
MOVED 24
YOU DREW ME 27
DEFINITION 30
A PICTURE WORTH A THOUSAND WORDS 31
VISION 32
I ASKED HYMN TO MARRY ME 35
HYMN 39
BURNT OFFERING 40
ALTERED AND ALTAR'D 41
VISITATION 42
INTERVENTION 43
MEM'RY 44
PREMONITION 45
KENNY RANKIN AND YOU 47
AFTER THE ASHES 48
PRESCRIPTION 49
AWAKENING 50
THE BODY REMEMBERS (PART 2) 52
PIECES (OF PASSION) 53
WORN 54
WOKE 57
FREED 58
PRECIPITATION 59

RISK 60
VENTilation/4 days in a row... 61
THE "EX" FACTOR 64
OVER YOU 65
I'M RAISING CHILDREN 68
IF I COULD SING 71
LISTENING TO DONNY (JACKSON) 74
THE BACK STORY 75
NIRVANA 76
3RD SET 77
BB REIGNS 78
DAUGHTERS 79
A POEM FOR MICHAEL & J 80
LIFE 81
I AM 82
3:35AM 83
GRIEF. STRICKEN... 84
EMBODIED 85
YOU ARE NOT ALONE 86
ONE LOVE 87
73. TUESDAY, JANUARY 19, 2016. 88
SACRED 89
EVIDENCE 90
AGENT 91
ELEVATOR MAN 92
CATFISH 93
COOKIN' [another mem'ry] 94
MORE SACRED 95
OUTTA CONTROL 96
PSALM 97
HYMNS THAT WROTE POETRY TO,
FOR/ABOUT ME 99
HYMNS IN THE FAMILY 100
ACE BOONS (PAST AND PRESENT) 101
THE MAGNIFICENT SEVEN 102

MY FAVORITE/TEACHING HYMNS *103*
ACKNOWLEDGEMENTS *104*

HYMN

There is but one hymn

One song

One love

For us all---

1st TESTAMENT

His voice was symphony
Album of the year
News at eleven
It forecast good weather and
World report from Africa to
Northern Cal
And stories like you wouldn't believe
And namesakes and treasures
That fall into your lap
And make you smile.
I know he writes poetry, 'cause he wears it
Like cologne ----
No, like holy water on a blessing
This reverent warrior
Son of a servant
He wears humble like a crown
And kindness covers him like indigo
On grandma's hands,
That seeps into your pores
When he touch you.
He breathes hope with his laughter
He, the smile of a new day
And the twinkle of the daughter
In his eyes.

WRITTEN ON THE NINE

What if love
Were the only way
To breathe?

HE SPEAKS

Between 3rd rib
The sun/son
And the space
Between
My words
He speaks
I hear
We dance
Seven-year itch
O' holy alliance
Spirit-orchestrated
Tango, has never been
Like this---
He holds me
Between
Thumb & index
Dabs me just
Behind his ear
I am amber
In his mem'ry
The scent of
His belief
Smells like
Jesus
Everywhere!
Lung, inspiration
There be no expiration date
Our shelf life's
Hymnspired

All breath
Be holy
But this breath
Be mine
Divine intervention
He drum daily
To my heart
And we sing
Each other into
Revelation
It is the revolution
We have been
Waiting for
It is the Love
The Damascus
HE SPEAK
Ovah me
Moves [our] generation next
To being born
Into their father's hand
And through their grandma's eye(s)
They look like Nana & Popi
All over again
And we be born again
Through the Gawd of
Second chances
And the love of "I AM"
Say, he speak
And it is done
Amin, Ase', Amen
And a Wombin.

UNDER A JULY SKY

Romanced by a prince whose
Kingdom come
In liquid passion & Abyssinian whole notes
Who don't stutter when he talk or step
But DO dance---
Grounded in original tongue
Plants feet like seeds about to grow
Into something real any minute
Sooner than you'd think
Then sprinkles hope onto the ground
For those who have lost their way ---
Doesn't ask for donations
Gets his in aces & spades
Runs Bostons every 15 minutes
Got super frequent flyer miles
'N' miles 'n' miles to go
Before he sleeps
He's been given thyme/time to heal
Uses it wisely & often
Tempers the bitterness of life
With sweet nothings whispered
In a 4-letter, 2-syllable
Long-distance song
Called Popi ---

SPRINGTIME

I had a massage the other day

Preparing my body for the new season

And you---

When you stroked my skin

As you often do

Said I'd been touched

By someone new

And although you didn't want to know

Who [he was]

Said you could tell

By the touch [he left]

That he loved me

As much.

RITUAL

Come in and let me wash the people off you
'Cause I don't want to sleep
With them tonight
Not with the children or the bills
Not the job or your ex-wives
And don't kiss me with anything
Else on your mind…
Not the fellas or the playoffs
Not the 5 o'clock news
I really only want to sleep with you.

COLLAGE A TROIS

I feast on my memories
When I don't wanna cook
Sip your voice
From long-stemmed glasses
Chilled like a good Chardonnay
And at dawns like these
They're poured in my hands to cleanse me
And spill over large coffee mugs with saucers
To catch the drip
I drink them like hot carob milk
In winter
And eat them like sweet rolls
For breakfast.

MOVED

Like wind move water
And Holy uses spirit
By music, laughter & time
By hugs & ceremony, I am moved
By bearded smiles 'n' tattooed styles
Of '50s diamond-ear & signified mouths,

Moved

By Ashford "or" Simpson, Syreeta, Nailah
& Mahalia, well I said "I wudn't gon' tell nobody
But... I couldn't keep it"
'N' Beah, being "One Is A Crowd" all by herself

Moved

After 25 years on a New York street, &
Back on the bus
I've been moved
All placentas buried; they're a palm tree now~
Moved by men who love their children
& wombin who love they mens
& babies who don't have to choose

Carried

Like a preacher moves through a sermon
With scripture wrapped around his heart
And woven into the fabric of his character

With truth, his collar & Gawd, his boutonniere

Changed

By the power of memory & forgiving
& scars that don't itch anymore (I am healed)
And the voices of reason I'm still willing to hear

Baptized

By Blk Sonshine & "Stage" presents
And pas des deuxs by phone
And Joshua sounds like… forever
By breath, mantra 'n' rain, doin' that dance

Shaken

By stringed instruments (voices included)
And 7.0 at 2 a.m.
And "nana, I am calling you"
And long-distance cell to let you know you are missed

Transformed

By grits written 'cross the page
'N' red shawls
By the rhythm of miracles that dance

In the streets

And poetry good enough to wrap my grandson in
I am so moved sometimes

I can't "speek" or spell
Tell the sun to move over
& bask in me for a while

Moved.

YOU DREW ME

Somewhere in the middle of the night

You drew me close.

Drew me like a pencil--

[A Carlos - Picasso – Gauguin - a Varnette

An Olu - Bearden - Charles White - Greenfield – Joysmith - Michael Brown,

And painted me like THE GOD paints the skies

Each day,

Complete with smile

And a glow that shone in the dark of

BEFORE the dawn.

Somewhere in the middle of the night

You drew me close,

And whispered nothing I could hear with my ears

So I had to listen with my heart.

Somewhere in the middle of the night

You drew me close

And drew my first breath as I drew your next

Not knowing where I left off

And you began,

Somewhere in the middle of the night

You drew me close---

Which wasn't close enough

And when I asked to stay

Found I really didn't need an answer

But when I had to leave

Felt I was leaving a part of me behind,

Somewhere in the middle of the night.

Somewhere in the middle of the night

You drew me close.

DREW ME LIKE A PENCIL

And painted me like THE GOD paints the skies

Each day

Complete with smile

And a glow that shone in the dark of

[The 5 o'clock] BEFORE the dawn.

Somewhere in the middle of the night
You drew me close
And whispered nothing I could hear with my ears
So I HAD to listen with my heart.
Somewhere in the middle of the night
You drew me close
And drew my first breath
As I drew your next
Not knowing where I left off
And you began

Somewhere in the middle of the night
You drew me close, you drew me close
You drew me close, you drew me close
You drew me.

DEFINITION

A hug is a physical exercise

Of humans

Involving forearms

Lots of time and space

With only GOD in the middle---

Directions for use:

Wrap well

Squeeze gently

And hold.

A PICTURE WORTH A THOUSAND WORDS

Hand placed like heartbeat on drum
Holds her shoulder
Like breath on silhouette.
(We stand in the middle of a rain forest
just for us
And right where we are it rains).
The moon is full & peers behind a cloud of palm trees
Dressing the sky,
Who's about to do a striptease & take it all off
To let her light shine.
Dimples on the East side of his face mirror her own
And the gap 'tween his teeth reminds her of a space
She's been waiting to fill.
Nose wide bridges to cross
And she a scene in the eye of his storm,
Asks him to come out
And play.

VISION

He rises from the sea
Like the steam of a natural hot spring
Direct and full of life
Hair glistening like BLACK DIAMONDS
In the noonday sun
Each carefully woven lock like the ROOT
Of a tall oak tree
Ancestor of the fruit it bears.
Waves of wonder
Liquid curls that gently caress
The MAGIC of his mind
Or an aerial view of the woolen rainforest
That protects his mountain crown.

His skin a yellow, golden, bronze, earth-brown,
MASAI-RED, deep, dark-chocolate, blue-black indigo,
MIDNIGHT SKY OF SMOOTH
Sometimes from head-to-toe
Eyes wide open, half-asleep, deep-set, dreamy
Almond-shaped, clear
And always watching out for you.
Teeth that sparkle with the brilliance of a seashell
On the seashore
Form a smile that's safe
Invites you in
To loving arms
Stronger than you'd imagined
Willing and able to hold   carry
Support and nurture you---

Gentle enough to hold a baby/child.
Connected from a place rarely seen
By the naked eye
His hands reflect the CONNECTION
BETWEEN MAN AND GOD; the touch of passion
The touch of love   the HEALING feeling
The science
The ART of making dreams come true
And visions possible.

LEGS that withstand the test of time
Walk or run   the 4-minute mile
Stand only on the ceremony
Of foundation
And FEET dance to the RHYTHMS
OF THE SAINTS   THE ORISA
THE GOD
Ready, willing and able to stand
Toe-to-toe
With ANY man
But not afraid to RUN
FOR A CAUSE.
Ears that hear a baby cry
In the middle of the night
HANDS that change diapers without
Turning on the light
VOICE THAT SPEAKS
With the power of the north wind
The softness of a summer breeze
Words that TEACH
Patiently.
Eyes [again] not ashamed to cry

That light up with DELIGHT
AT THE SIGHT
OF YOU
Lightning-quick thoughts race
Through his mind
Manifesting visions
From the DIVINE
LIPS that kiss the ground you walk on
Hands not afraid to till the same
LISTENS INTENTLY WHEN YOU SPEAK
HONESTY AND TRUTH HIS MIDDLE NAME
Brings you a rose but calls YOU the flower
Stays with your children, for hours and hours…
KNOWS that his place is right where you stand
THIS IS MY VISION of an AFRIKAN MAN.

I ASKED HYMN TO MARRY ME

TWICE...

HE NEVER SAID

NO~

HYMN

There are people who love me
I don't even know their names
But they hug me
With the corners of their smiles

There are children not from my skin
But of my roots~
As mother & friend
I attend their most important rituals
I am invited
We are attached
I call them mine

There is a place
Where love grows by the doorway
& honor lights the room
& laughter witchu or atchu
Is the anthem for which we stand

And there is a man
Who sings when he breathes
Heals when he whispers
And when he prays,
And when he prays-
God listens.

BURNT OFFERING

She receives
His gift
And they laugh
Shares a blessing
He knows she'll
Love
And they laugh
Slips his scent
Into her pocket
To keep her safe
While he is gone
It isn't funny
It's just nice
So they laugh.

ALTERED AND ALTAR'D

Left
Standing
At the altar
Just means
You supposed...
To kneel.

VISITATION

The parlor---in Ms. Rosa's favorite chair he sits.
Facing a fireplace where nothing's burned for years
He is warm. Embers from grandson's last visit flicker---
Will go out soon, but not before SHE comes.
The front door's BEEN open. Entering his world like an
Old friend, expected, she crosses the threshold of his
Southern comfort
And he IS comfortable, for he is at peace.
It looks GOOD on him. All accolades and titles, folded
Neatly and put away.
Eyes closed in some pre-meditation, there is rest for his
Weary.
Not wanting to disturb this silence but acknowledge the
Presence,
She crosses her fingers, crosses her heart, then the room.
Leaning into his air space,
Bowing like a congregant, she whispers her kiss to his
Brow.
Holding dress to her chest, so as not to ripple his mood
She removes her lips,
Still bent on his behalf
And before her ascent,
His crown touches her heart
And lips, not far behind
Kiss her chest
Like THE KA'BAH
His hands, welcome her home.

INTERVENTION

They were both frightened.

She tried to NOT love him

Then realized [that]

She wanted him

More

Than she didn't want

To love him

And that GAWD

Wanted her to have him

MORE THAN THAT.

MEM'RY

I used to fall
Into his eyes
And there...
He'd catch me

PREMONITION

He came just to TEACH in my life
Just around MIDNIGHT
A minister a message a miracle waiting to
Happen
Said, "I AM...`a method'
Your morning your breath of fresh air"
He brought what I'd asked for
With no ulterior motive
Came w/his heart in his hands embracing my spirit
Set my soul on NICE
Walked in w/FREEDOM 'round his neck
& a pocket full of dreams
Came to heal my heart set the soles of my feet FREE
Accepted my offerings asked for NO THING in return
Nothing I was unable to give.

He is spirit child come to visit his mother
Take good care of her---
Speakin' in her garden he watch her flowers grow
'Cause he knows the secret life of plants
He is response-able man not afraid of LIES
'Cause he sleeps w/the TRUTH
EATS w/the TRUTH
Speaks w/the TRUTH
A man child All his life he BEEN to the RIVER-
From ALABAMA forests DEEP in his MEMORY
To Jackson Avenue sidewalks paved against their will
He been a man-child ALL his life ---
Been a REST to the weary

Been a SOURCE of the NILE
Between beard & locks there be
EUPHRATES in his smile
He is the left hand of GOD working righteousness
On the NIGHT SHIFT
A lion in winter w/a Capricorn heart
He is a prophet w/non-profit status
Plays BOARD GAMES w/the UNIVERSE---
Pyramids planets stars w/o stripes.

He is mountain man come down from the mount
Whispers rainbows in my ears gonna
TEACH ME how to pray---
He come EARLY Sunday mornings BEFORE the sun do
Rise
Speaks to me of secrets in the middle of the night
Brought me FREEDOM in a feather CAUSE I'd forgotten
How to FLY---
He came just to TEACH me
That I'm the teacher in my life.

KENNY RANKIN AND YOU

There is no poetry for this.
Loving you by degrees
Hotter than July in January
No matter that it's winter.
Cool as mint juleps in back porch
Summer's sarong---

There ain't no poetry for
Feeling you between sheets of
Hmphs and moans
Addressing you in protocol
To keep the temples between us
Familiar
Being touched by man and Gawd.

There ain't no poetry for
Lovers' energy being transferred
Between friends
Walkin' around about to burst,
"Simply explode is a lot to hold"
What am I gonna do...
What am I gonna do, now???

AFTER THE ASHES

There weren't enough tears
There weren't enough tears
So we just stood
And danced
In the rain.

PRESCRIPTION

Because we heal
One-in-other:
"Breathe me in
And call me
In the morning~"

AWAKENING

I.

I awoke
His hair between my teeth
My breath in the palms of his hands
I wiped the smiles from his eyes
And brushed his promises
From my hair   blinked
And they all fell into a neat little pile
On this bed of   on fire
Ready to be sacrificed for more
Powers of persuasion than I already had.

I was looking for HONOR
But wasn't ready to lie to get it
(Where is the honor if there is no truth?)
So I took the path less traveled
Found myself   out on a limb   by myself
Had climbed so high   couldn't back down
(You can back down from a lie but never from the
TRUTH)
I couldn't back down
So I plunged into the river where truth
Runs deep
Then jumped into the air where truth's
The ONLY current
And then I learned   to fly---

II.

I sleep with my hands tied behind my back
To keep from reaching out for you
Put a fork on my tongue
To keep from calling your name
I put a meter on my mind
So thoughts about you
DON'T EXCEED THE LIMIT
I sleep with a CHAIN around my heart
To keep from loving you
Too much
Then dream of my heart singing
UNCHAINED MELODIES
Old lovers never DIE
They just TRY to KEEP IN TOUCH
Someday, we'll all be free.

THE BODY REMEMBERS – (PART 2)

My skin
Just flew in
Yesterday--
My heart is still...
In the
South
East
With my memory--
Passion-steamed
Frosted glass
Lips
Committed
To warm-
Refreshing,
Reminiscence,
Laughter
And the humor
Of arms.

Didn't know
I'd become
Southern bell...
Judging from
The reverb
I'll always be.

PIECES (OF PASSION)

He came to me in summer
On Pocono rain
With Africa in his hands
& October on his mind.
In synchronicity
Took me to the river
Held me up
Washed me down.
His bitters--sweet offering
Healed me with embrace
& juice that makes me wanna
Bring back the veil---
Knows the purpose for
My mouth & hands---
Said so.

A wish 'cross time zones
Distance, sun & moon
He speaks to me of waters' edge
& deep.
Creation is his heartbeat
He prays in public with his art
When sun kiss my imagination
With dew---
I feel him at dawn.

WORN

He wears me like an amulet
Worn close around the neck--
My breath a tourniquet   keeps his heart
From falling out   his chest
He wears me OUT   in public places
With private glances   from yesterdays
Searching for me   in his TOMORROWS

He wears me WELL
Like finely tailored suit   silk in left breast
Pocket
Alligator SEE YA LATER shoes
That don't need shine
He be wearin' me OUT y'all
First wore me DOWN...   gently   like
Diamond stylus needle   that fit my groove
'Til I was...smooth
WORE ME DOWN with
CAREFULLY NAVIGATED STARES
That led me to believe   on 33 1/3
It's my turn
And now he wears me UP to his neck in wishes
That nights would be longer
And daze never end
He wears me well
Into the flava' of the music we hear and others
Don't
WELL, into the absence of obsessive behavior

He wears me OUT   to lunches and dinners
Where passion flavors nourishment

Like water for chocolate
And the fountain of the youth that runs through our
Veins
And the fountain of our juices tastes just the same

Wears me like DEEP DISH COBBLER AFTER
Family feast
Never uses toothpick just keeps sucking his teeth
Wears me like mother's milk on baby's breath
He wears me WELL
Like COLTRANE on a Blue Note
Black-leather-pleasure on a Friday night
By Ohio Players IKE or Barry White

Wears me like a token of your affection
Like rose petal on softness
Syllable on syntax
Like May-meets-December-in-the-middle-of-June

Wears me like the smell of
FEAR-MOANS ON FULL MOON

Wears me like the fine of an overdue book

Wears me like the FINE of take-a-second-look

Wears me like a memory that you never forget...

Like silver lining on moon full mornings
Mournings when grief's the only silence to be heard

And when he takes me off
And lays me down before he preys my soul to keep

He wears me well into submission
Before we fall asleep.

WOKE

When WAKE UP CALLS…
THAT we answer
Is more important than
HOW we answer.
WHEN SPIRIT SAID: "WAKE UP!"
I knew it was speaking to me---
(I was the only one in the room)
Then whispered, "About this man you call,
"Home-skillet" …
"PATH-OLOGY… is NOT the STUDY
OF THE PATH!"

FREED

I thought I'd rather sleep w/you
Than to sleep w/anger
Truth is, I'd rather sleep
Alone.

PRECIPITATION

WEATHER you know it

Or not

Life is a condition:

Though clear skies are present,

Be prepared

For rain.

RISK

If ever you lie to me again
I will rip you from my heart
To be free of you
And risk bleeding to death
In the process.

VENTilation/ 4 days in a row...

DAY ONE:

Orgasm has never been a substitute for

The TRUTH.

Comparing the two---TRUTH feels better

And lasts longer

DAY TWO:

I am not impervious to pain

Just 'cause I've shouldered a lot of it

I'm learning to cry TODAY when I hurt

Not tomorrow after I've thought about it,

And I can't worry about saving face

When my soul is at stake.

Our relationship's surviving on LIFE SUPPORT

Not breathing on its own

Remove the I.V.'s, I no longer want you

Under my skin

Instead, I'm willing to submit to daily doses of
Reality, honesty and truth---are you?
No longer willing, and fast becoming unable
To tolerate
Pieces of me holding onto pieces of you
And calling all those pieces whole.
Been chasing you so long I been run down.

DAY THREE:
When passion turns to power
You can say to the man
You've loved/ love/been loving
That orgasm is no longer an acceptable
Substitute for the TRUTH---
Denial, no longer an easy river to swim in
The undercurrents running so subtly before
Now too strong, homicidal
Giving fair warning no more.
I used to not mind waiting
While wading in the sea of

"It'll get better soon."

I've grown tired of having patience

With a patient that gives no indication

The remedies are having an effect.

DAY FOUR:

It's REVOLUTION TIME!

Two years after LA's insurrection

I engage in revolutionary tactics

To save my own soul---

Saving my body 'fore my mind's too old

To remember what I been told:

"Girrrl, take better care of your Self

Than anybody else" and "Other people

Only treat you like you treat you!"

The Revolution is ON and ORGASM

Will never be a substitute for the TRUTH!

THE "EX" FACTOR

She tells the "ex" [that]
She hopes he falls in love with someone soon
So he can leave her alone.
Tells him: "hope you fall for someone as hard
As all the women have fallen for you…
'Til you can't see straight!"
His reply:
"What makes you think I haven't already?"

OVER YOU

I been over you---many times

Breasts in your mouth

(Your hands on my back)

Nourishing you with my

"All I ever needed was you"

On my breath

I been over you alright.

Like gravy over Real Cutlets 'n' Rice

With them greens and Putaat on the side

The kind you gotta special order

From Venela's Vegetarian Soul.

Like the volleyball going over the net

Only to fall prey to a player about to hit it

One mo' time like a roach too small

To smoke

I been over you alright.

Like burning embers raked over

Hot coals

Waiting for the sacrificial lamb

To grace the space between flame and sky

Yeah I BEEN over you

Thought I had to

To get from under your spell---

But getting over

Ain't all it's cracked up to be

It's the getting THROUGH that's true

It's the TEST that's the best

It's walking through fire getting singed

Coming out alive

Transforming survival skills into a

Living art

I been over you alright

Bent over you   like a slave

Been a fool for ya baby

Bent over so you could

Kick your heels three times

Right in my ass to keep me home

I bent over you too long

So long [that] it hurts to stand up

But I'm beginning to

Stand up for my SELF

Stand up for my health

Stand up for my rights

(That's all I have left)

While you've been resting on your

Laurels

Sheilas and all the other sistahs

Who ain't stood up--

But I bent over you a long time ago

Been over you a long time ago

I been over you

And it's alright!

I'M RAISING CHILDREN

I'm raising CHILDREN

I'm NOT the farmer's daughter

Raising CHICKENS

To be slaughtered

Not the sharecropper's child

Raising CANE to be

CUT DOWN

I'm raising CHILDREN here

RAISING

Not California singing dried fruit

Raisinettes

Not raising STRANGE FRUIT

To hang from some oppressor's tree

I'm raising PRECIOUS fruits

To grow HIGH on the vine

PRECIOUS FRUITS reaching toward

The sunshine

Raising the fruits of my womb

To multiply   by fives

To stay alive

I'm raising CHILDREN HERE.

No little Bo peep

Leading her sheep to be slaughtered

These are my daughters

These are my sons

I'm raising CHILDREN y'all

Raising them UP

ABOVE the flood waters

I AM the crossing guard

Cross me and YOU'LL be sorry

'Cause I'm raising CHILDREN here

Between rock and hard place

Betwixt slim and none

'Tween fatback and no slack

I'm raising CHILDREN y'all

The instructions are included

DON'T FOLD, SPINDLE OR MUTILATE

The instructions are included

DON'T FOLD, SPINDLE OR MUTILATE

The instruction's BEEN included

DO NOT FOLD, SPINDLE, MUTILATE,

NEGLECT, MISUSE OR ABUSE

Just follow the instructions

Like you do OGUN OSUN and the MOON

Just follow the instructions

'Cause I'm raising CHILDREN here

I'm raising CHILDREN y'all

I'm raising CHILDREN here.

IF I COULD SING

If I could sing
I would sound like Dwight Trible
Awaiting notes that rise
Like the sun before dawn
To fill up a midnight
With a sky-full of stars.

If I could sing
My songs would HEAL
Like Aretha's DOCTOR
And Stephanie's I FEEL GOOD
All over
Same song would heal like the ACQUAH
MAN himself
Just need to touch you
Don't need herbs off the shelf.
If I could sing
My voice would be THE CURE
The A.M.A. couldn't patent
Wrap bandages around your wounds
Like Ella or Sassy when they scattin'.
My voice would echo album covers filled
With DREAMTIME melodies
Heal ya like James Brown
When singing please please please.

If I could sing
My songs would FEED the world

Serve you syncopation on silver PLATTERS
Sprinkled with Phyllis
Dianne Reeves a la carte
Prysock and Eckstine
Your choice of entrée
Tossed with Horace Silver
Garnished with Andy Bey
Dessert would be sweet
Like Luther or Nancy.

If I could sing
I would sound like Dwight Trible
An Oasis in the middle of your mirage
That wets whistles and lips
And the dried bones of our histories.
If I could sing
I would sound like
DREAMS forming in new minds
And memories of Divinity.
If I could sing

Hearts wouldn't need no strings
Hairs wouldn't need tweezers
No plucking would be allowed
If I could sing
I wouldn't need no Grammy
And American music could keep their
Awards
If I could sing
I would hold you like the whole notes
Rahsaan Roland Kirk wouldn't let go of.

If I could sing
I would sing our people AWAKE
Our children into safety
Our men into honor
Ourselves into our rightful place
Among the women who've created
WORLDS
With just the mention of their names
If I could sing
I would sound like Dwight Trible
And the world would say
ASE'.

LISTENING TO DONNY (JACKSON)

He read
Right through me
Then left his water
In my hands...

THE BACK STORY~
We met in high school, not middle or low... I don't recall just when because he always felt like family and resembled my uncle Larry. If I told you what he "have done fuh me" it would take "some time"... If I told you how it changed my life, it would take forever--- there are voices that ground and surround you, then respect and protect you.

The Rev. Dr. Nirvana Reginald Morgan Gayle "force", is that one.

NIRVANA

The
Garden
Demands
[That] we be
Flowers!!!

08.19.2016

Celebration of life
4:00pm
Direct transmission

3RD SET

The healing journey
A trip for your mind
Pack up all cares
Leave the trouble behind.
Could be "Bumpin' On Sunset"
But the road
Will be smooth
The bass makes you dream
His guitar makes you
Swoon---
The piano tickles your fancy
And drum
Jumpstarts your heart
The Ron Muldrow Quartet
At 5th Street Dick's
A precious work of art.

BB REIGNS

Even the skies couldn't take it.
Pouring their hearts onto us
Already DRENCHED IN stunned
We, wet with the BLUES of the pain in his art~
The KING who BAPTIZED A WORLD
WITH OUR WOE
Dethroned by a coup too sweet to resist,
The HOLY TRINITY NOW A WIDOW
NAMED,
LUCILLE.

DAUGHTERS

[We]
Don't bury
Our fathers
But lay
Their soles
To rest
Among those
Whose
Legendary feats
Defied
The marks
Called time.
Release
The hands
Tethered by
Training wheels
And witness
Their realignment
With the stars.
Relinquish
Our hold
To the boldest
Expression
Evidenced
Throughout
The existence
Of form
LIGHT
And SOUND.

A POEM FOR MICHAEL & J

Love is the safest place on earth
Protects you from summer's storm 'n' winter's pain
Love is the only neighborhood to live in
These days...
Love cools you by day   warms you at night
Makes music when you exhale into her ear
Whispers sweet nothings on a regular basis:
"Enjoy your heart. Enjoy your heart. Enjoy your
Heart."

When you smile at each other---remember the sun
& the breath you breathe.
When you feel like you slippin' "Just touch the hem   of
Her garment
And be healed."
When you feel misunderstood
Just look into his eyes & inhale the seasons of your
Collective remembering
"Your telepathy will get his attention."

Create new memories for your tomorrows
Erase old yesterdays that just take up space
Each new day is now your forever
& forgive Gawd for taking so long
But know, She's always on time.

LIFE

The journey can be
The longest mile or a
Vacation
The search
A maze or a treasure hunt
It's all up to you
If you continue to breathe
The sweetness will pull you through
Will guide you
As you continue to breathe
The sweetness will become you
When you continue to breathe
You will learn
That the last sweetness ain't really
The last
Just the one before the next
So I continue to breathe
And I remember the sweetness
Whether I can taste it today
Or not

I AM

Being torn
From the
Shackles
Of resistance--
Bathed
By a man
Who gives me
Water
As a
Parting gift...
I am
Loved
And
Being love
In this
Time
Of cholera
And
My tears
Turn this
Fever
Into prayer.

3:35 a.m.

It still amazes me
That just when I think
There are no more tears
Then it begins
To rain.

GRIEF. STRICKEN…

Been searching the web

To find something

To laugh at,

To take this pain out my gut

Lump in my throat

Gag out this choke.

Surfing the net

I been working without

I feel like I've fallen through

Cracked…

The king has no horses,

The king has no men,

And I feel I shall never

Be put together again.

EMBODIED

I miss you
Like
"Everybody's"
Business~

YOU ARE NOT ALONE

From
The
WORD
There
Is
BREATH
From
Breath
Comes
LAUGHTER
And
In
Laughter
GRIEF
DOESN'T
STAND
A
CHANCE!!!

ONE LOVE

This man is mine,
Gawd gave "this" man
To me...
And this one, and this one
And this one.

73. TUESDAY, JANUARY 19, 2016.

17 years
Since the first
ALMOST
5 1/2
Since you
Left
And I'm
STILL
Writing poems
ABOUT YOU...

SACRED

I am blessed
You are blessed
Together
We are holy.

EVIDENCE

We both left the house
Ashen--- the oils from
Our bodies having been
Drunk   by the sheets
Of earlier morning cover---

He spoke of memories I'd thought he forgot
I basked in the power of the sweetness I
Sometimes/ often forget he has.
He spoke of holding me as I slept
And before we parted, shared some fruit &
A kiss that was even sweeter---

Helped me start my car & as I drove away w/a smile,
Seeing him smile, I thought to myself---
I have no intention of bathing away the evidence---
I want the world to know he loves me.

AGENT

I didn't know
He was
FBI---

He didn't know
I was
WANTED.

ELEVATOR MAN

Alleviates the pain
Pushes
HOT elevator buttons
Feeling his way
From one floor to another
Expectations rise & fall
Lets you down easy
Elevator man does it all---
1st floor   2nd floor   next stop
Mezzanine
Shifts your consciousness gently
His manner is SO clean
You wonder where you're going
Then wonder where
You've been
The Elevator Man
Has struck again.

CATFISH

Late last night
She fried catfish
And stood
Wrapped in a blanket
From her son's bed.
A man approached,
Told her she was lonely –
Been without a man
Too long.
"No good woman like you
Should be a monk,"
He said.

COOKIN' [another mem'ry]

We were...
At the kitchen
Sink
I was...
Almost
Down the
Drain
My back...
Palm tree
In the
Sway
He had...
All of me
This way
Behind us...
Brown rice
In a pot
Exploding...
Somehow
We forgot.

MORE SACRED

We didn't make love
We made LIGHT.

OUTTA CONTROL

I had to pull over
After leaving his house
Because I couldn't
See straight/
That kind of want.

I wanted
Whatever
# of babies
He had left/
That kind of love.

Pregnancy is a
Communicable disease
I was willing to contract.
I asked hymn
How he felt about
Being wanted "like that"
He answered in smiles,
Poetry and music…
Then he introduced me
To his mom.

PSALM

"How DARE you love me like you mean it?
Honor in your intention,
You bring laughter to my heart
And my cup runneth over & over---
Again.
Because of you,
I live in a place where
The scent of star lilies
& white roses
Renegotiate air~
Handle me like,
"Baby, I'm for real."
Okay, I know I asked Spirit for this,
Just didn't know
It would be here so soon…
A bucket full o' brothas
Got me flashin' like
Railroad crossing ---
How dare you love me like GAWD sent ya?
Just cause 'e did---
Told you things about me
I ain't admitted to myself,
Told youse so you could help me
Heal…
"This" is what love look like
From the inside
Of a spirit who says,
"You mine, all the time."
Of a Gawd that love you like

Always ain't never been defined,
Just is…
"Don't you know I ain't used to this?"
But when you open your heart
Your eyes will follow
And lead you to me every time,
"How DARE you love me like I
Deserve it?
Watch me,
Let you!!!"

HYMNS that wrote poetry to, for, or about me [in order of appearance]

John Brake
Joseph Lamar Harris
Louis Gregory Cooper
Philip George Brown
Shareef "Abu" Abdullah
Les McCann
Msadiki Gray
Abiodun Oyewole
Cedric James Hinson
Hannibal Tabu
Conney Williams
Hiram Sims
Charlie Becker

HYMNS IN THE FAMILY

Father--Charles Magne Flagg Sr.
Grandfather--Roosevelt Ennis Sykes
Uncles—William Simon, Booker T., Rudy, Harold, Maurice, Larry, Richie, Raymond [Sykes]
Brothers—Valdez Magne Flagg, Charles Magne Flagg Jr.
Sons—Adekoye Shabazz, Akinloye Shabazz
Nephews: Tau Flagg, Jared Flagg, Jarel Flagg, George McDonald
Grandsons—Zuberi Williams, Omar J. Campbell
Godsons—Jamal Muhammad, Hodari Muhammad, Jorge Monterrosa

ACE BOONS (PAST AND PRESENT)

Curtis Robertson Jr.
Peter J. Harris
Gerald John Anthony Gregory Wilson
Frank Abraham
Glenn Brown
Newell J. Sherrod
Kenny Williams
Jabali B. Starks
Robert Davis
Daniel Bryant
Brian Shelton

THE MAGNIFICENT SEVEN

Joseph Lamar Harris
Louis Gregory Cooper
Philip George Brown
Shareef "Abu" Abdullah
Msadiki Gray
Poetry
Cedric James Hinson

MY FAVORITE HYMNS:

Cheo Jeffery Allen Solder
Khalid Delaney
Sadikifu Mfuasi
Purushattama Hickson
Akahdahmah Jackson

TEACHING HYMNS:

Dr. Leon O. Banks MD
Dr. Irwin Miller MD
Dr. Paul Fleiss MD
Dr. Jerry Rabow PhD
Mr. Burt Smith
Mr. George Cambouris
Mr. Nick Stewart
Mr. John Riddle
Mr. Michael Feinstein
Mr. Richard Fulton

ACKNOWLEDGEMENTS

The greatest gratitude goes to:
My brother Valdez, who first called me a poet, then led me to Stanley Lewis' Transcendental Meditation Introductory Lecture, that cleared the way for my creativity; Harmon Outlaw, who taught me how to write myself right out of writers' block; the late Rev. Barbara Bendaw-Williams, who encouraged me to do this 40 years ago; Peter J. Harris, Kambon Obayani, and Derrick Gilbert, who first published me, along with El Rivera and Pam Ward (who published me often), encouraged and got me plenty of reading gigs. Kamau Daaood and the late Billy Higgins, for founding The World Stage, my "chu'ch" every Wednesday since '92, giving me a place to connect, develop and spread my wings; the Anansi Writers Workshop and my dear Sister, Sequoia Mercier who led me there and her consistent Love and support; TiOva Padron, Jaha Zainabu, Ruth Forman, Oduanla Sangode, Tchikonsase' Aje', Nyesha Khalfani, S. Pearl Sharp, Ariah Tradition, Lady Gardner, A.C. Lyons, Michael Datcher; Family: Portia Moore, Karen McDonald, Nina Flagg, Pearl Williams ; my sistahs from the beginning: Carmen Freeman, Gayle Jewel and Jean Copes; daughters, Zuri [in the spirit], Iyabo and Oye [in the flesh]; Food4Thot, Love, Queen Socks, Eternal Mind, and AKoldPiece for your ever-present, EVERYTHING; Syreeta and Swamini Alice Coltrane Turiyasangitananda, who showed me how sweet and sacred a hymn could be; Rickie Byars Beckwith and Rev. Michael Bernard Beckwith for holding me with your Friendship, Music

and Ministry; Conney Williams, for coordinating this WORDship with me all these years; filmmakers, Alile Sharon Larkin, and the late Melvonna Ballenger; Special thanks to Hiram Sims, Nadia Hunter Bey, World Stage Press and The Community Literature Initiative, for your gifts, time, energy and patience; to all the poets on earth; to Yuri Hinson, for loving me, ushering your father into my life, and to Cedric James Hinson, for willing to be HYMN~

V. KALI

A 58-year East coast transplant to Los Angeles with a love for cold weather in her veins, V. Kali lives and breathes as a Poet, writer, actor, vegan chef, calligrapher, mother, Nana, healing agent [midwife, doula, Reiki practitioner, massage therapist, nurse], and taught Transcendental Meditation for 25 years. As a performance artist V. Kali has graced the stages of the Getty Museum, Grand Performances, House of Blues, Agape International Spiritual Center, Catalina Bar and Grill and most recently, the 2015-16 season of Center Theater Group production of THROUGH THE LOOKING GLASS at the Kirk Douglas Theater. She has lectured at Cal Arts, UCLA, USC, and produced the 2014 tribute, "Be Out of Heaven by Sundown, Niggah", to Poet Wanda Coleman. Original member of the Inspiration House Poetry Choir and Coordinator of the World Stage Anansi Writers Workshop, her work is published in numerous anthologies, including Catch the Fire, Super Girls Handbook, Voices From Leimert Park, her chapbook, Poetry is an Act of Peace (2012) and the book Messages From the Heart (2015).